Christmas Jazz

Arrangements by Tom Huizinga

ISBN 978-1-4950-6595-8

HAL•LEONARD®
CORPORATION

7777 W. BLUEMOUND RD. P.O. BOX 13819 MILWAUKEE, WI 53213

Visit Hal Leonard Online at **www.halleonard.com**

All I Want for Christmas Is My Two Front Teeth

Words and Music by Don Gardner

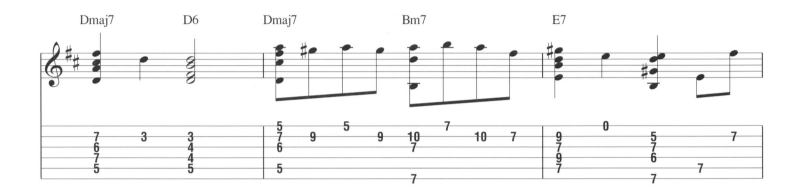

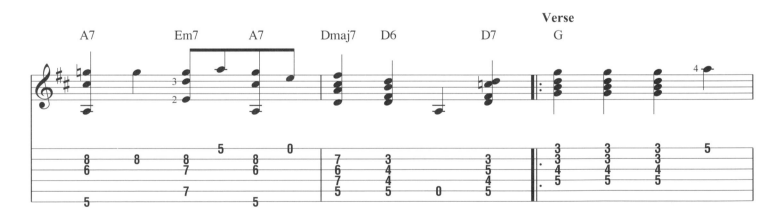

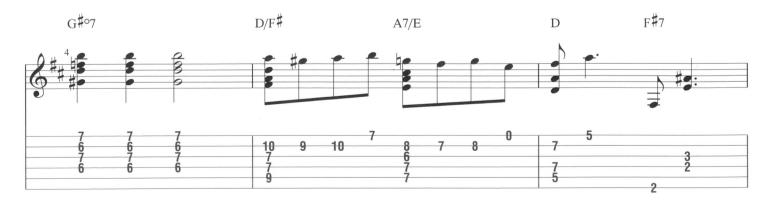

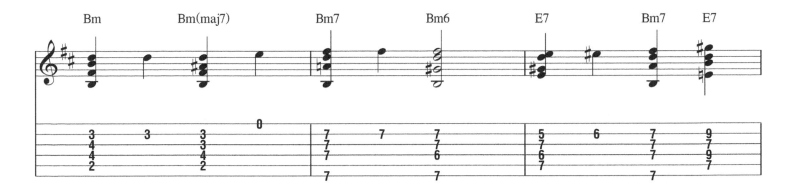

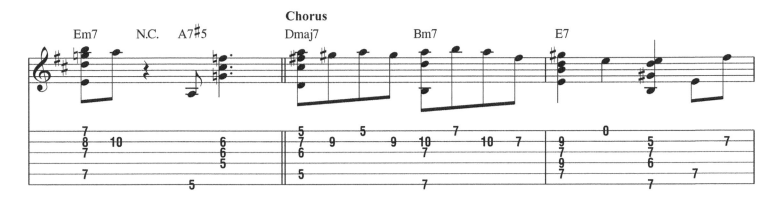

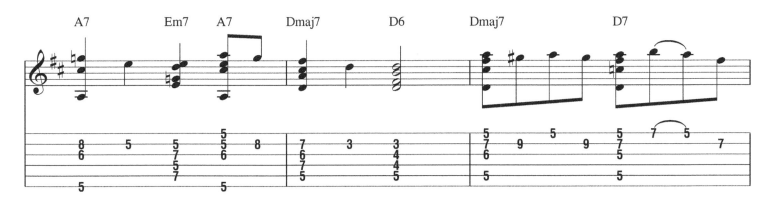

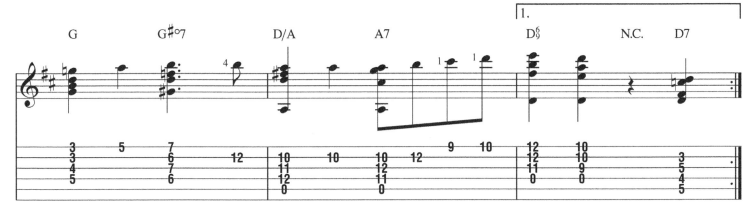

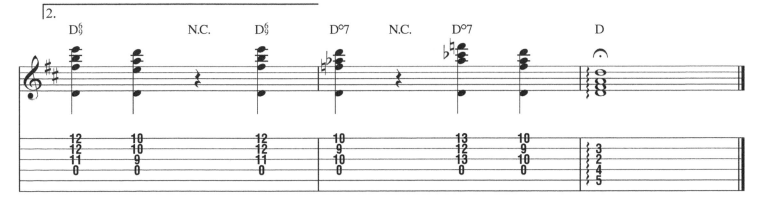

Auld Lang Syne

Words by Robert Burns
Traditional Scottish Melody

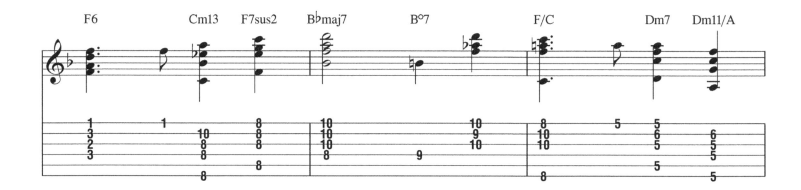

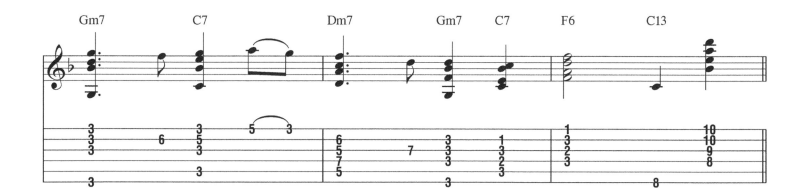

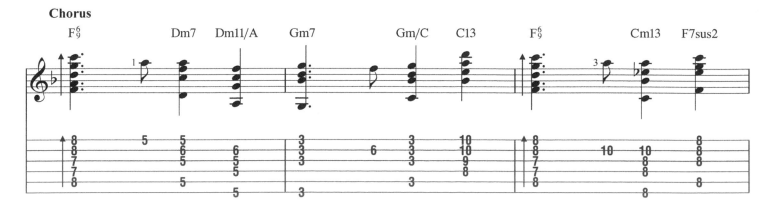

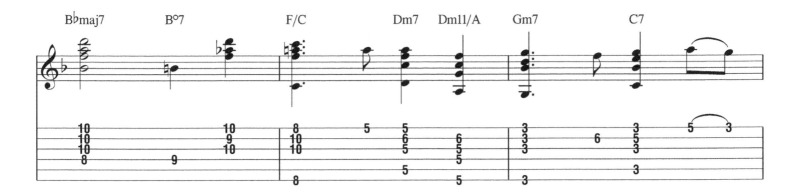

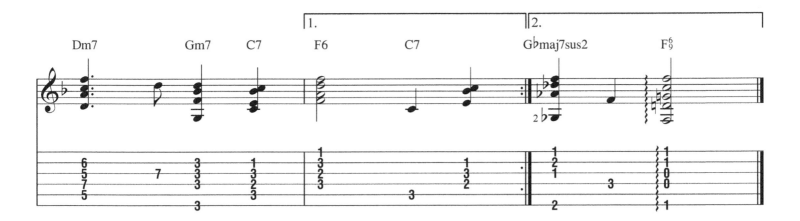

Baby, It's Cold Outside

from the Motion Picture NEPTUNE'S DAUGHTER

By Frank Loesser

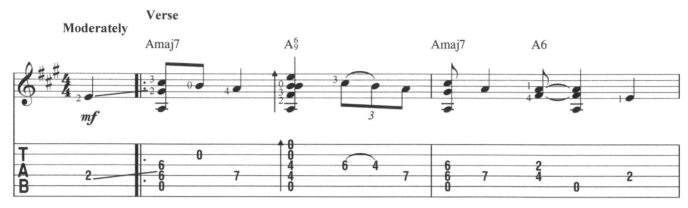

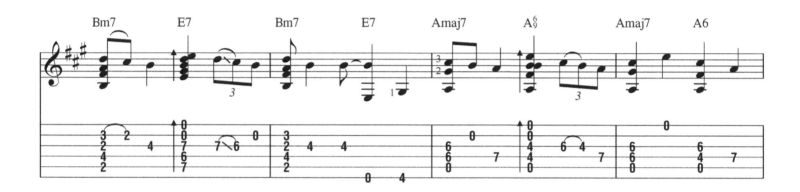

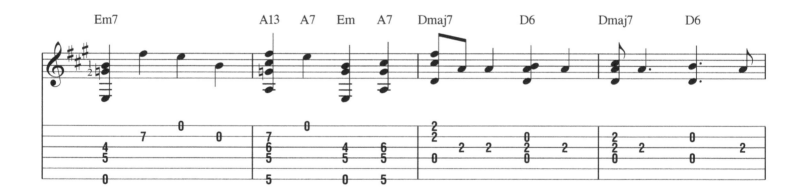

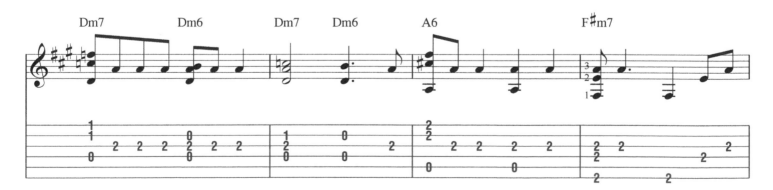

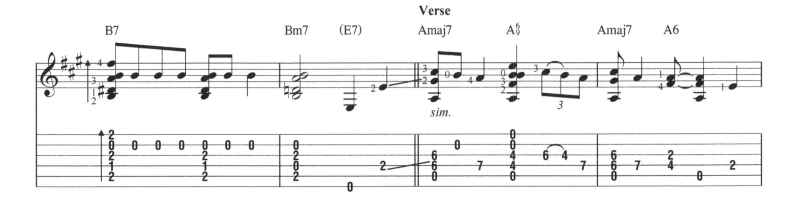

Verse

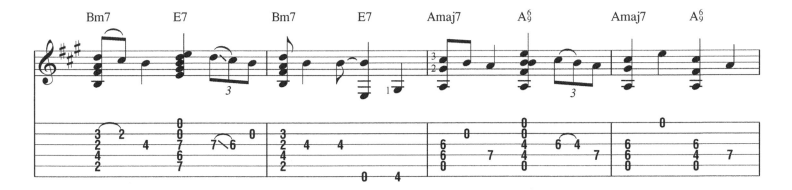

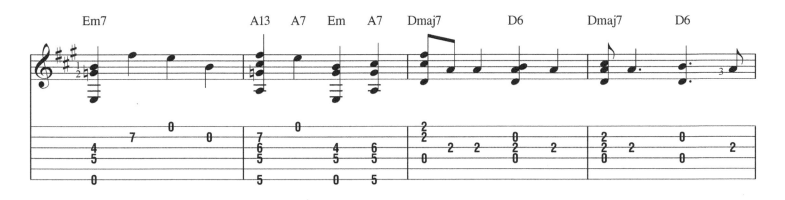

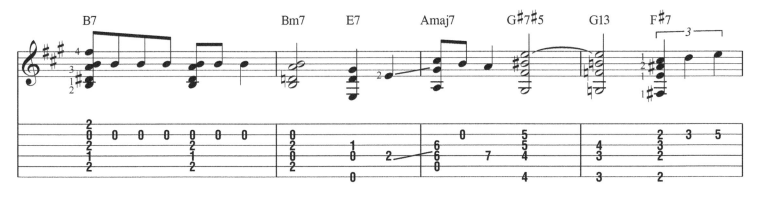

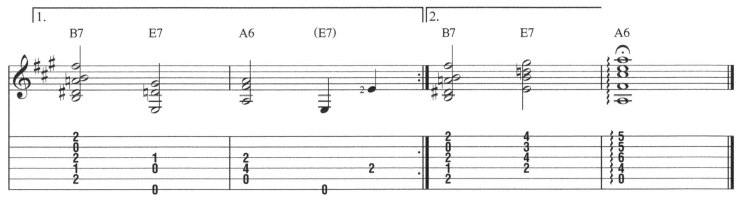

Caroling, Caroling

Words by Wihla Hutson
Music by Alfred Burt

Moderately slow, in 2

Cool Yule

Words and Music by Steve Allen

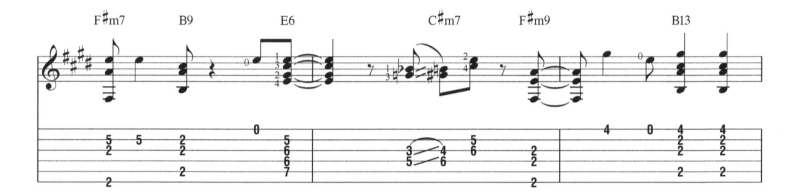

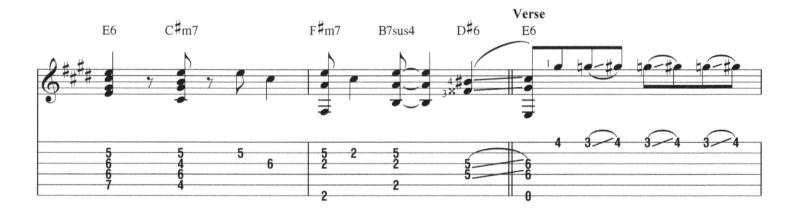

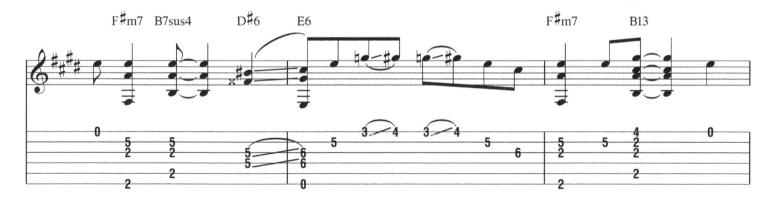

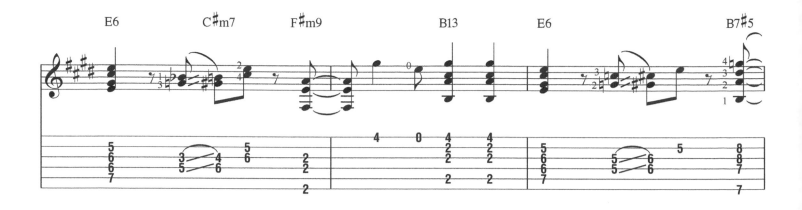

Bridge

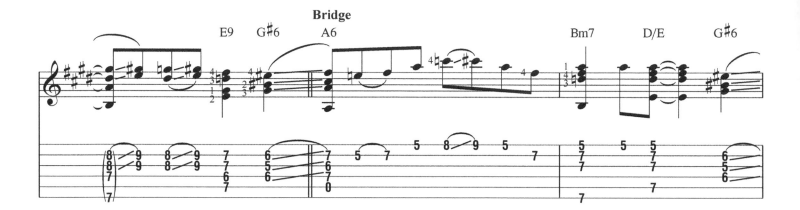

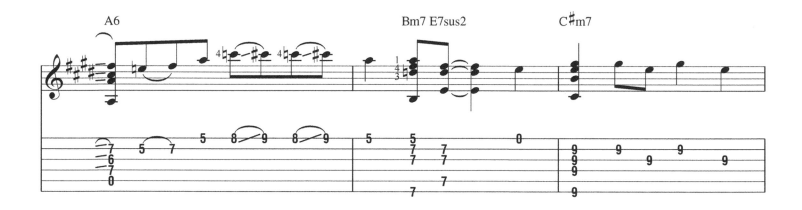

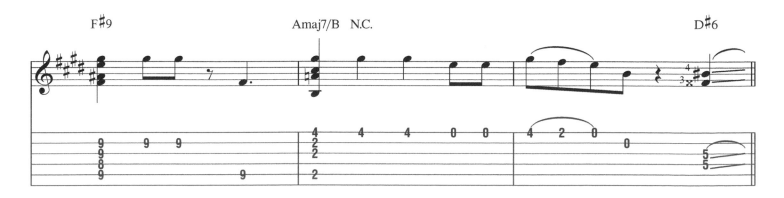

Verse

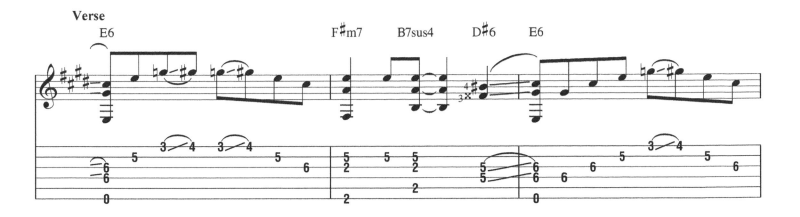

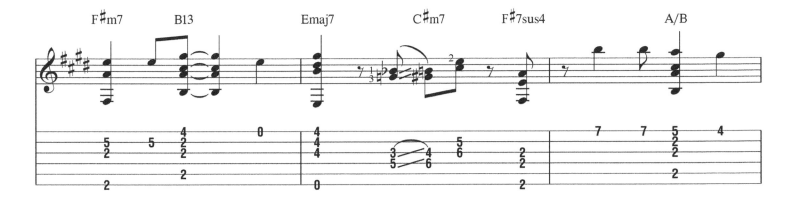

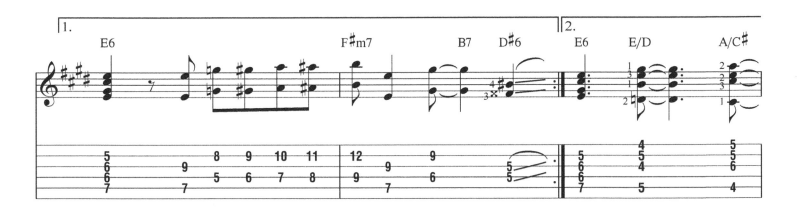

The Christmas Waltz

Words by Sammy Cahn
Music by Jule Styne

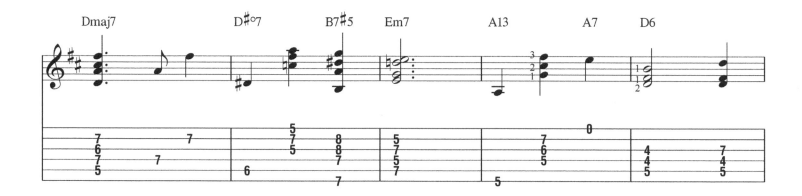

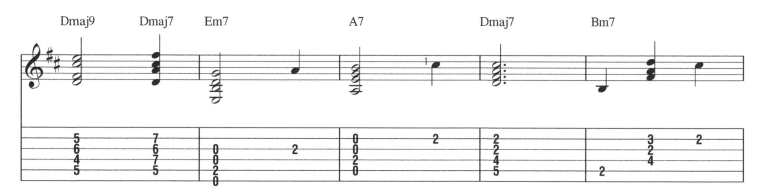

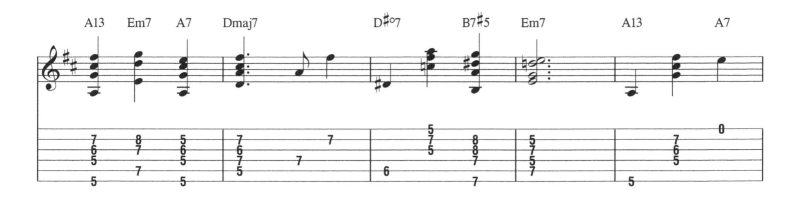

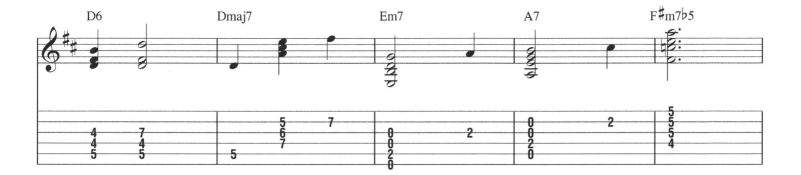

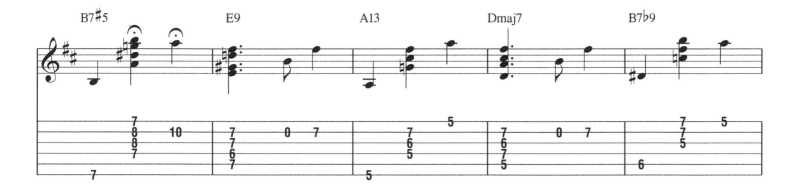

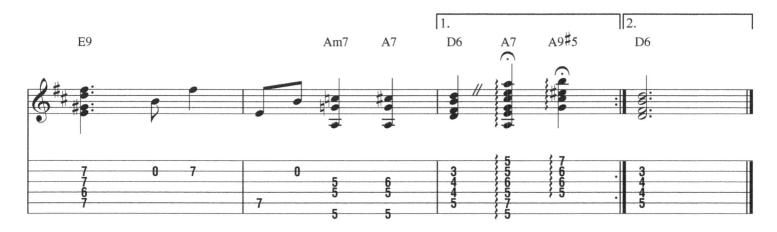

Happy Xmas

(War Is Over)

Written by John Lennon and Yoko Ono

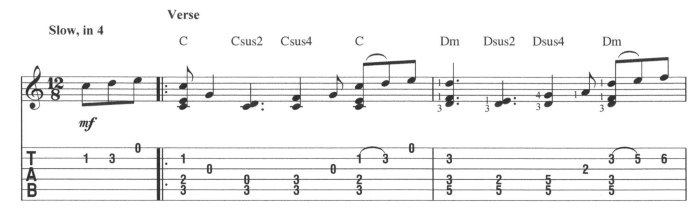

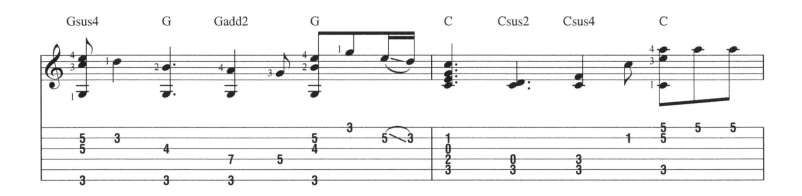

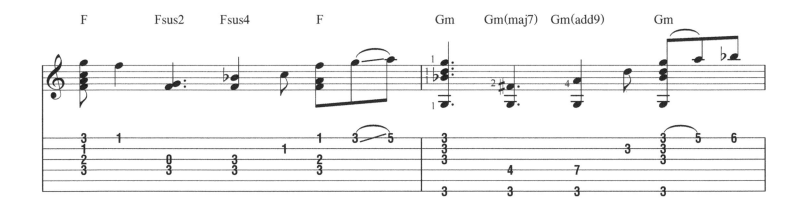

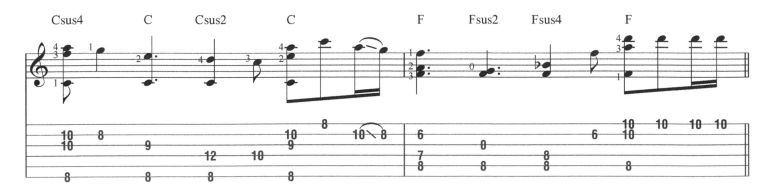

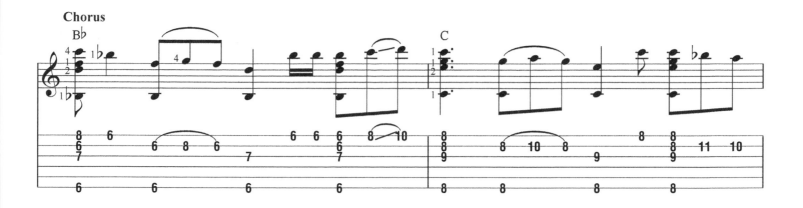

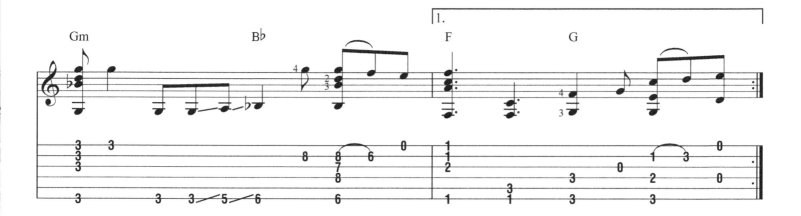

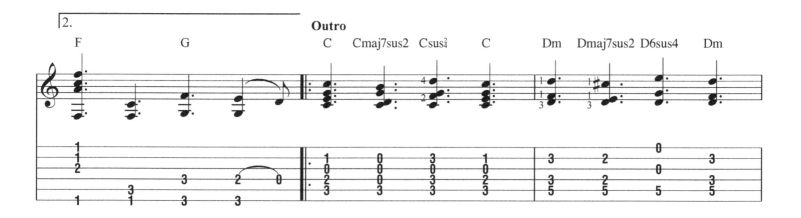

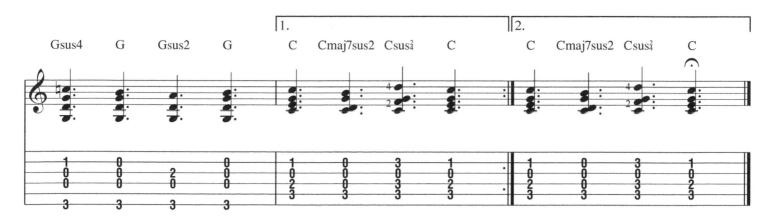

Have Yourself a Merry Little Christmas

from MEET ME IN ST. LOUIS

Words and Music by Hugh Martin and Ralph Blane

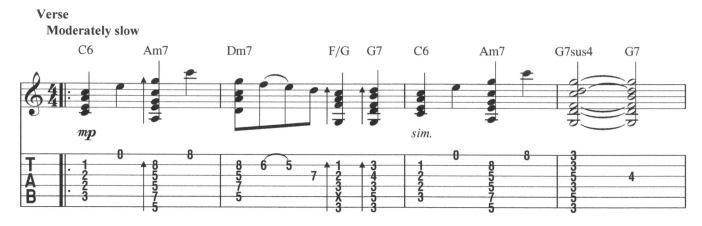

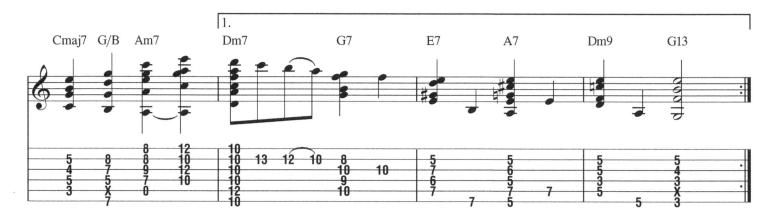

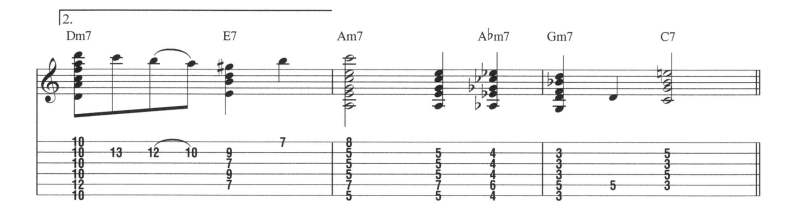

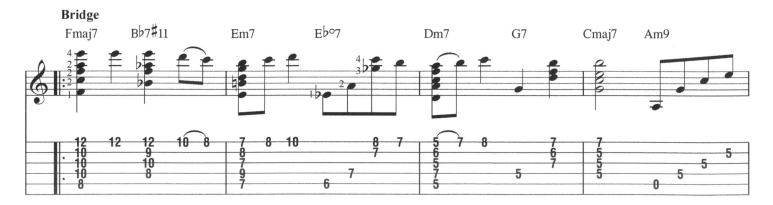

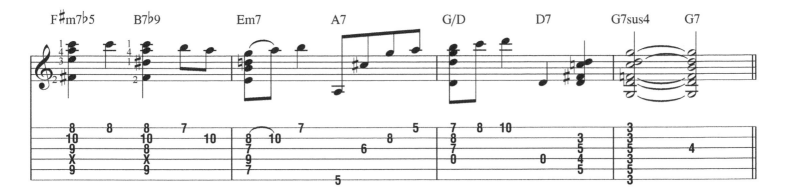

Verse

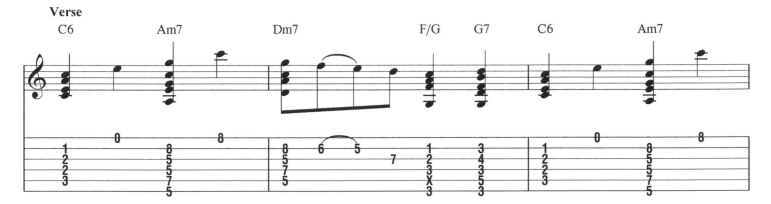

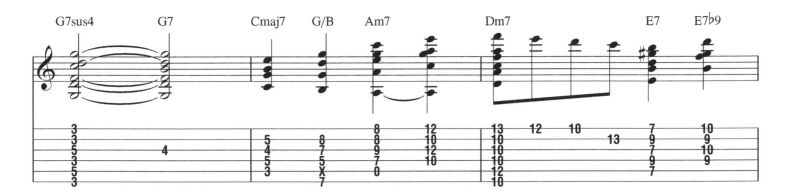

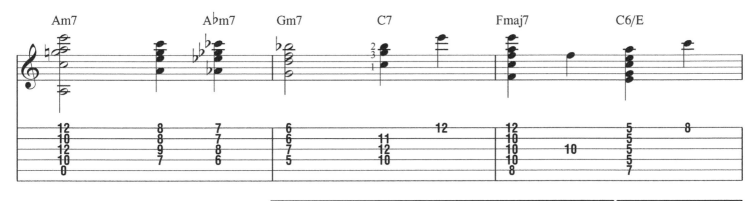

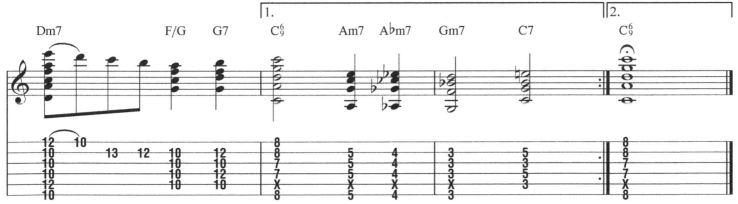

I Heard the Bells on Christmas Day

Words by Henry Wadsworth Longfellow
Adapted by Johnny Marks
Music by Johnny Marks

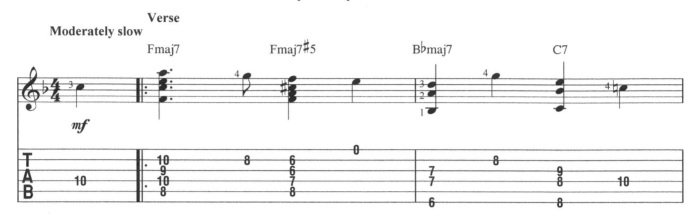

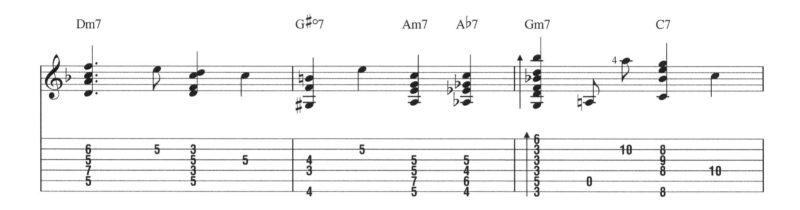

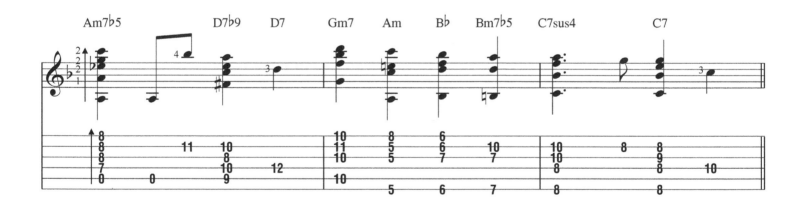

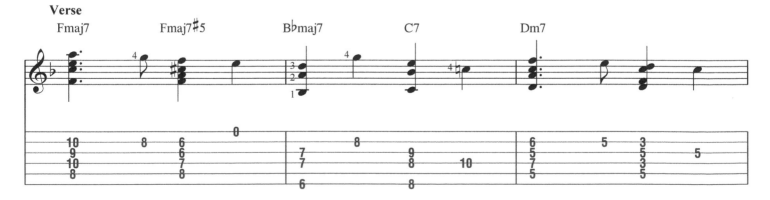

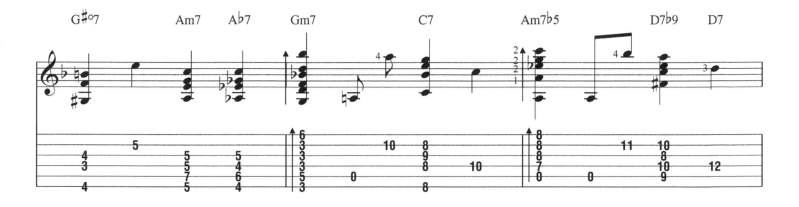

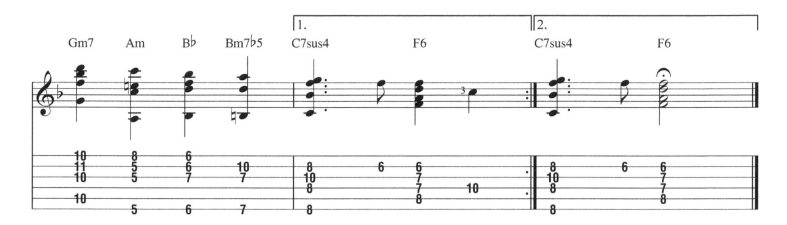

I Wonder As I Wander

By John Jacob Niles

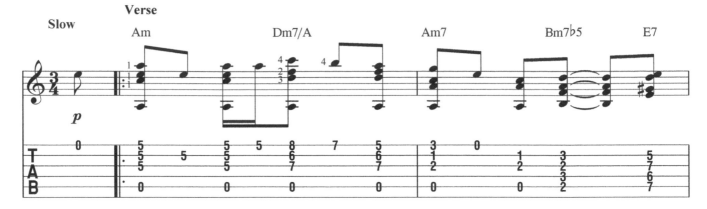

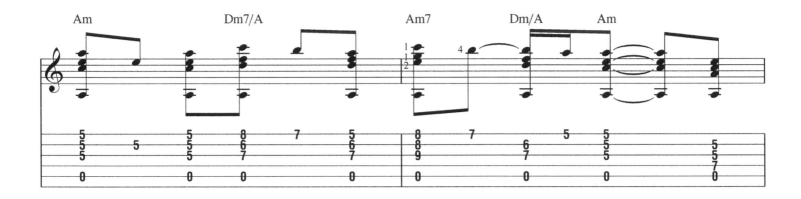

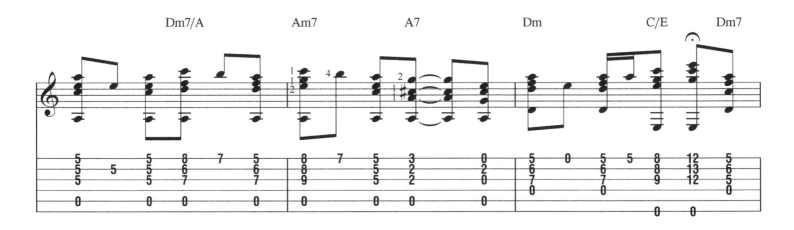

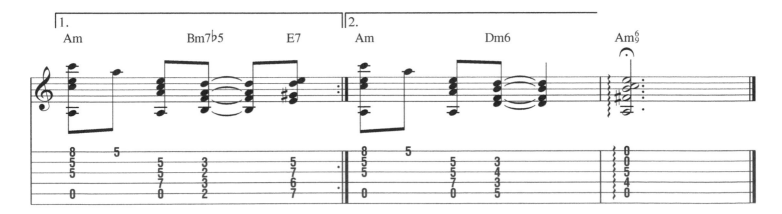

Mary, Did You Know?

Words and Music by Mark Lowry and Buddy Greene

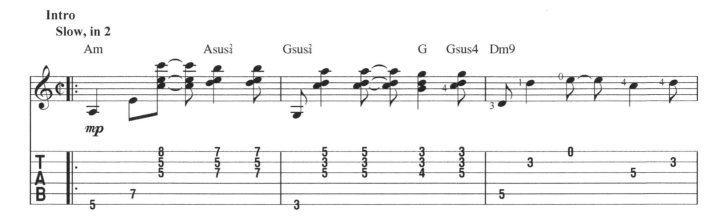

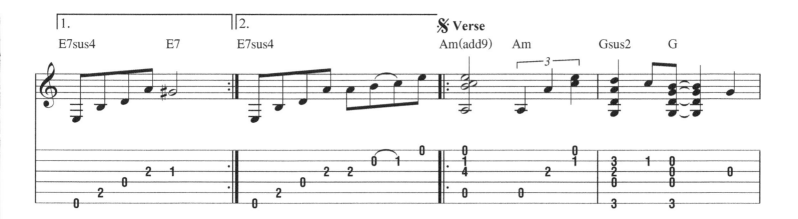

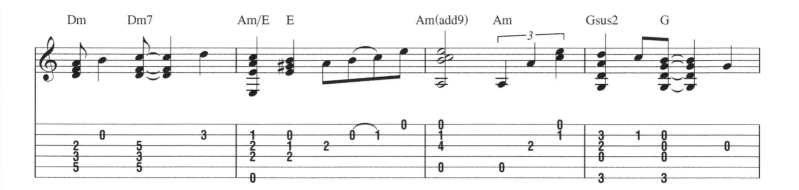

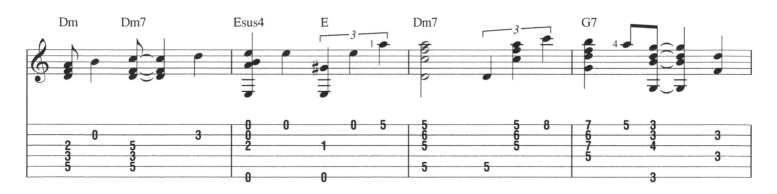

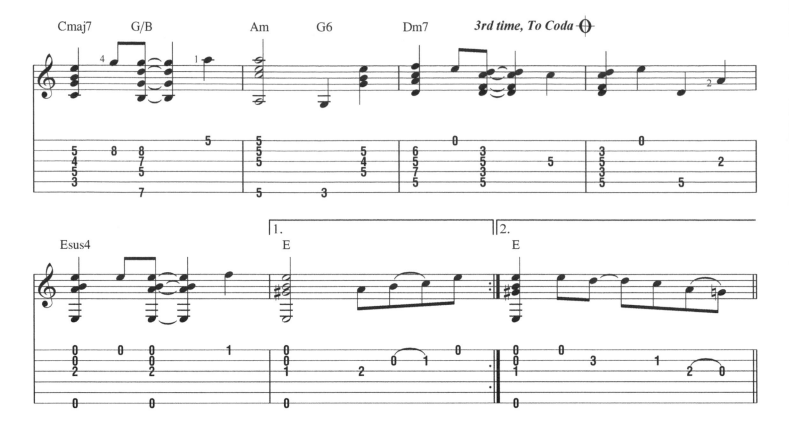

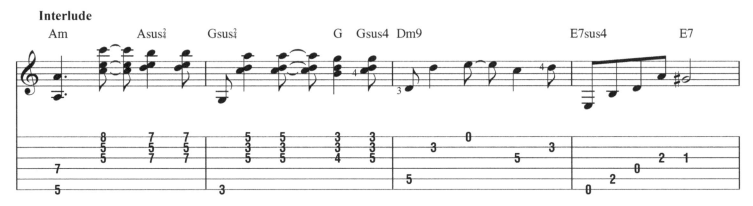

Interlude

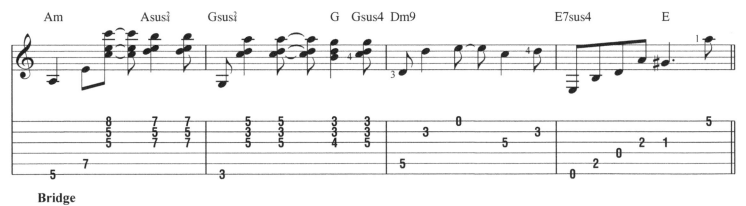

Bridge

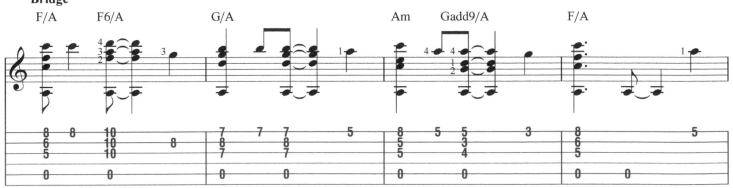

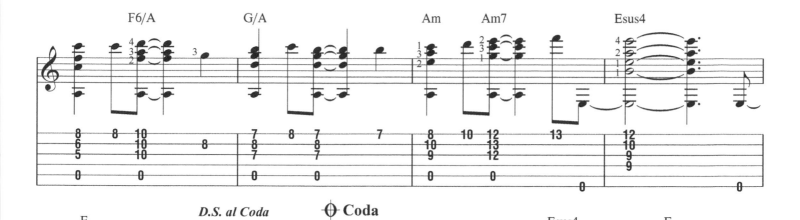

D.S. al Coda ⊕ **Coda**

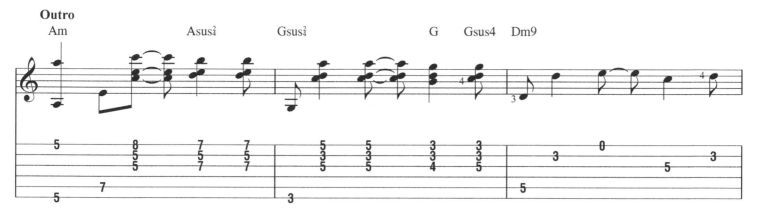

Outro

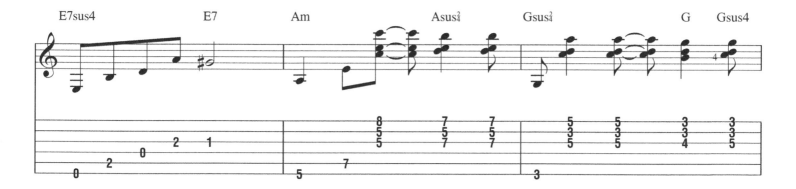

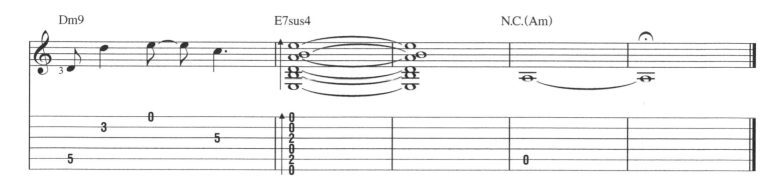

I've Got My Love to Keep Me Warm

from the 20th Century Fox Motion Picture ON THE AVENUE

Words and Music by Irving Berlin

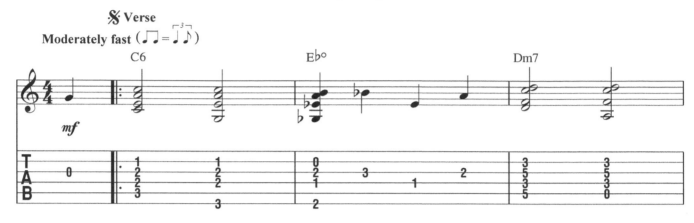

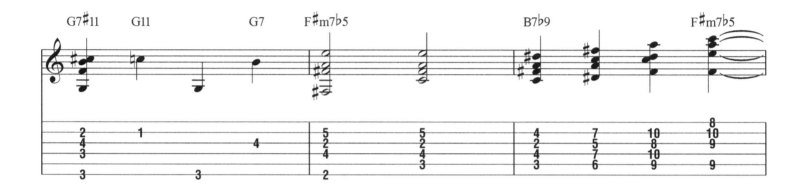

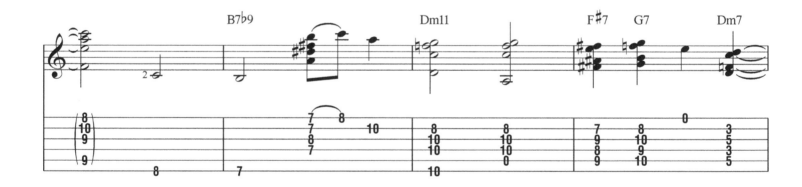

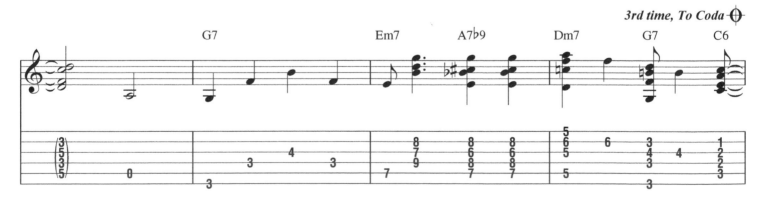

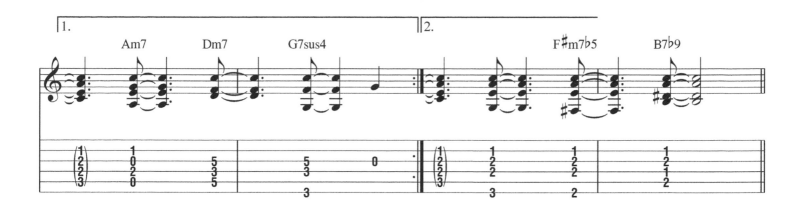

Bridge

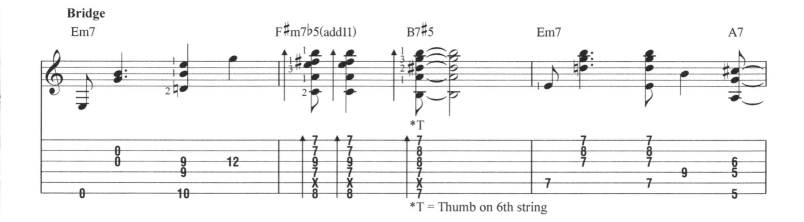

*T = Thumb on 6th string

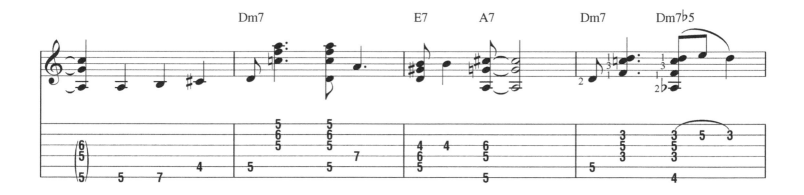

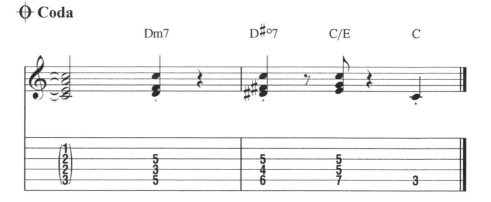

The Little Drummer Boy

Words and Music by Harry Simeone, Henry Onorati and Katherine Davis

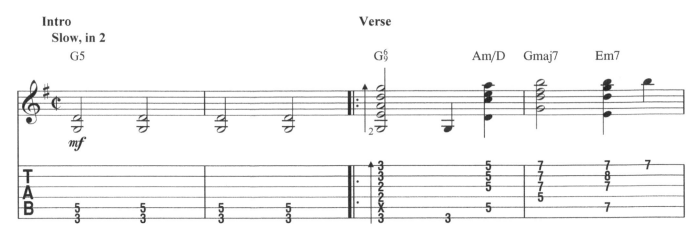

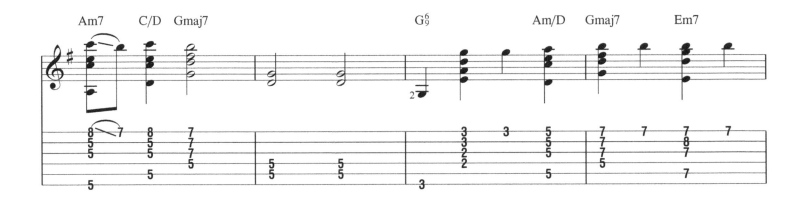

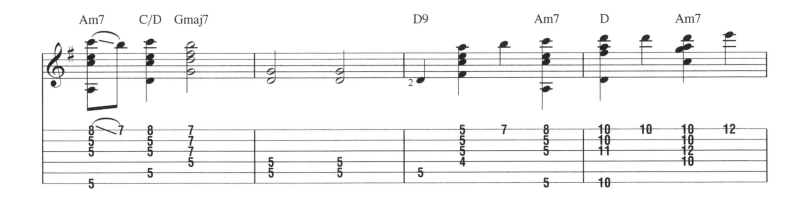

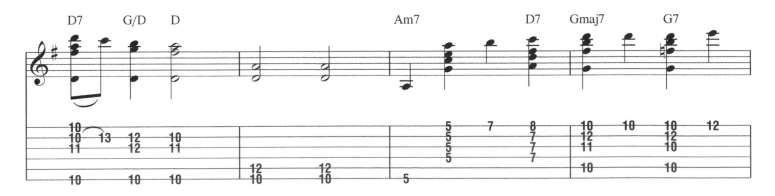

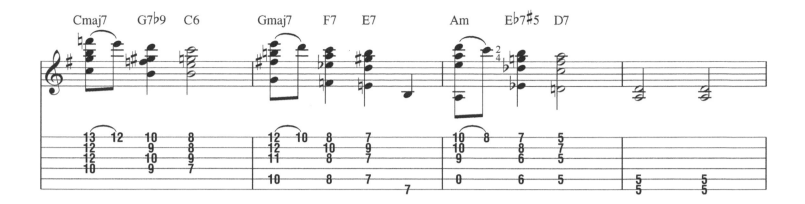

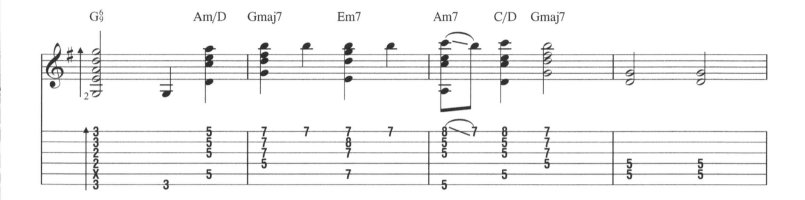

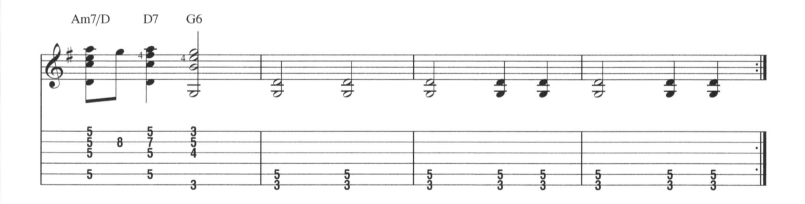

Outro

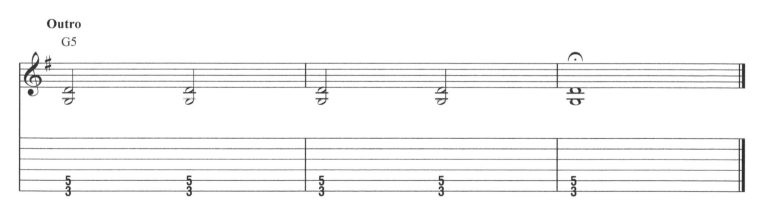

O Tannenbaum

from A CHARLIE BROWN CHRISTMAS

Traditional
Arranged by Vince Guaraldi

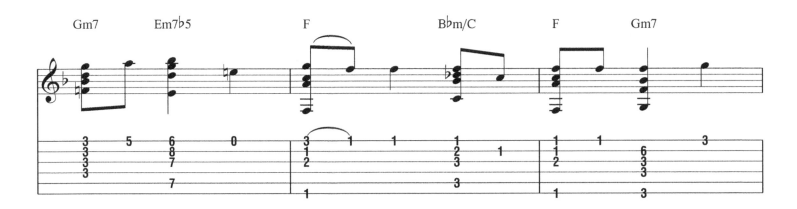

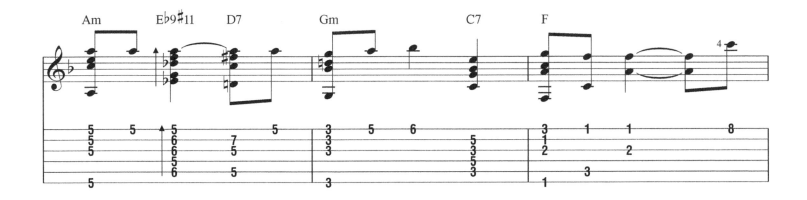

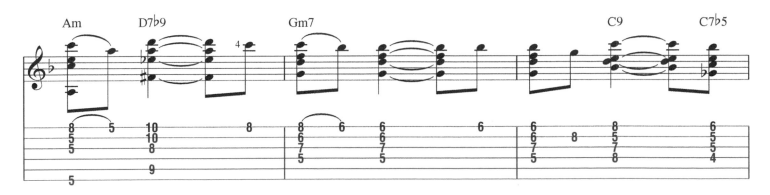

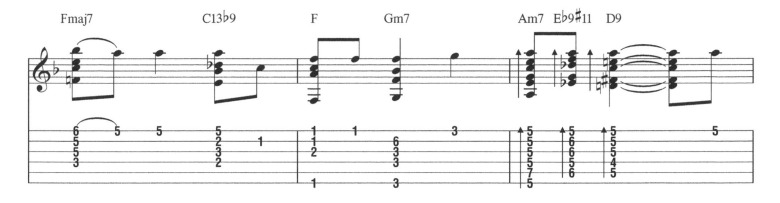

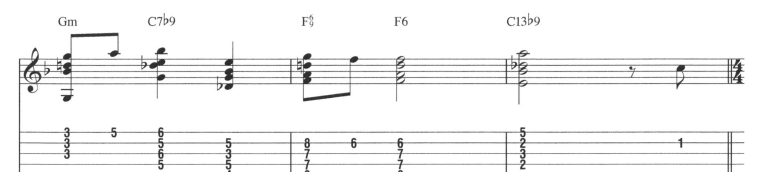

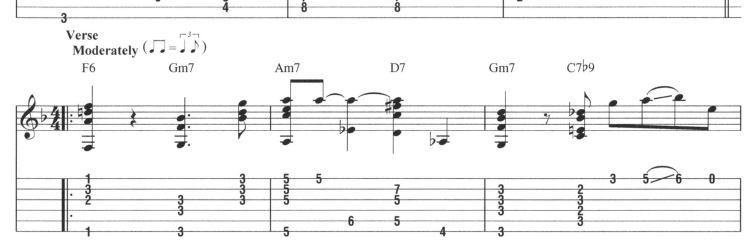

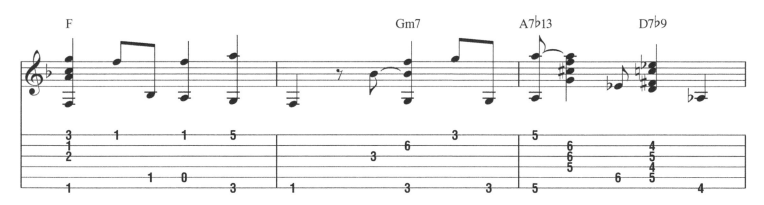

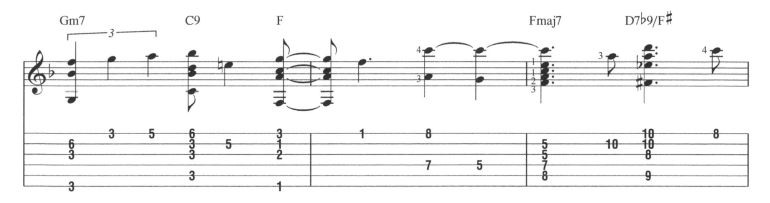

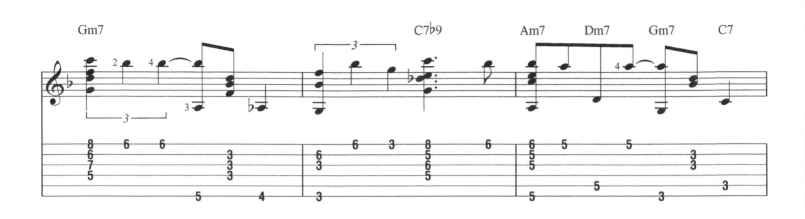

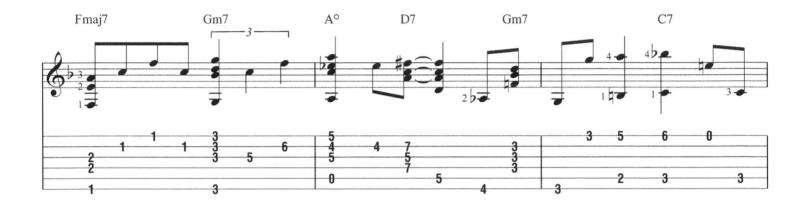

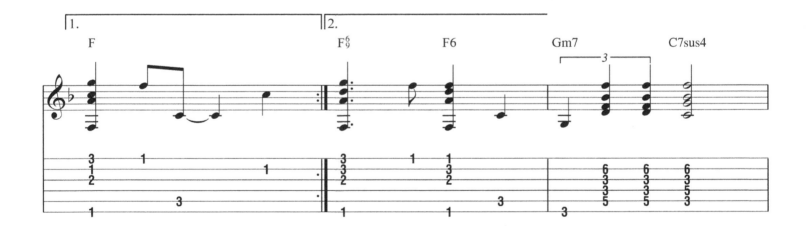

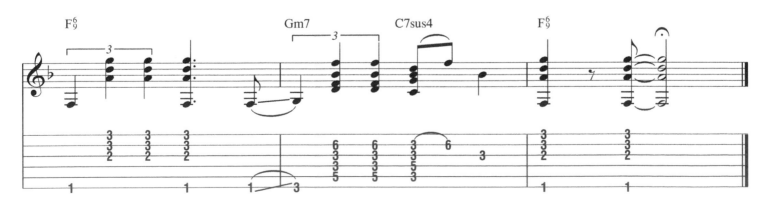

Santa Baby

By Joan Javits, Phil Springer and Tony Springer

Intro

Moderately slow

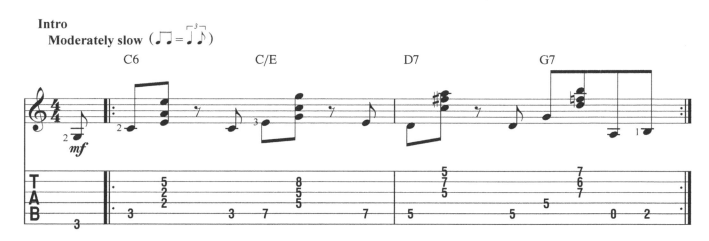

Verse

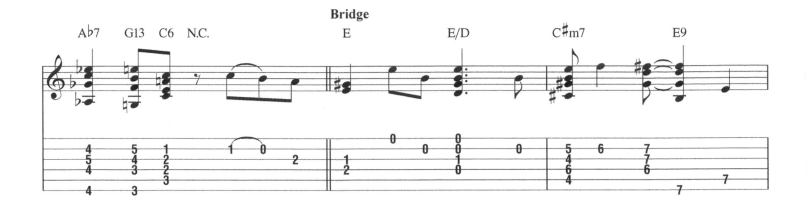

Bridge

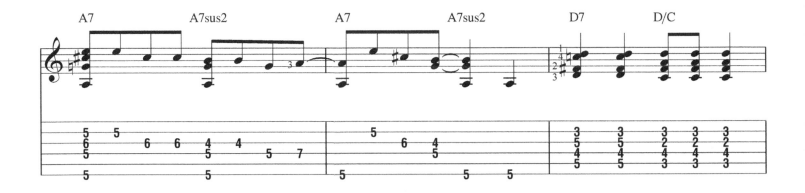

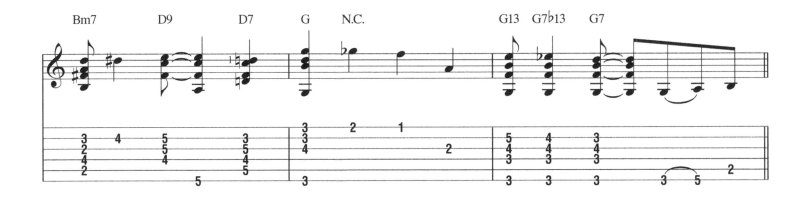

Verse

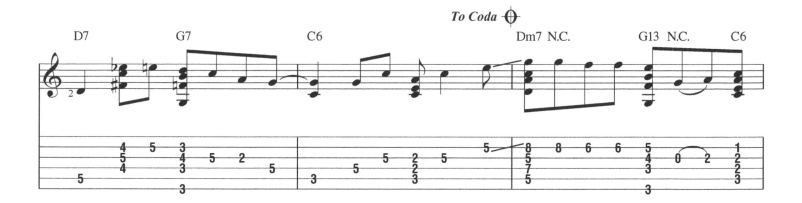

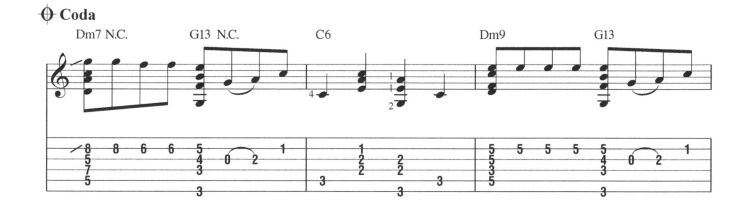

Skating

By Vince Guaraldi

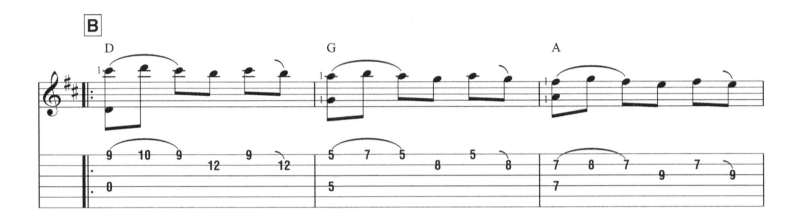

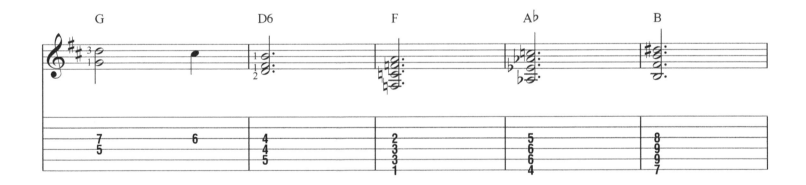

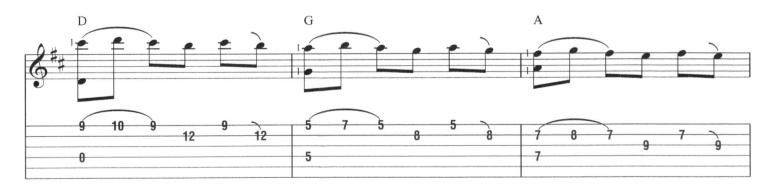

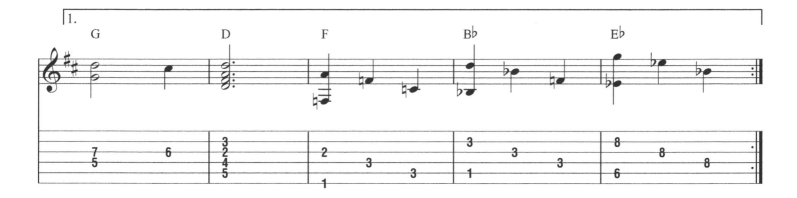

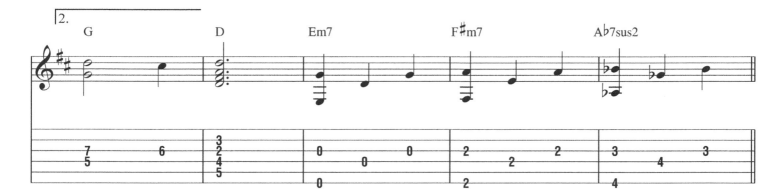

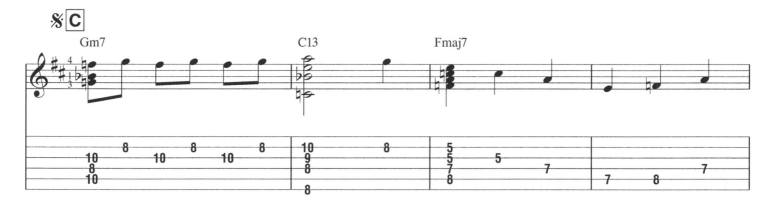

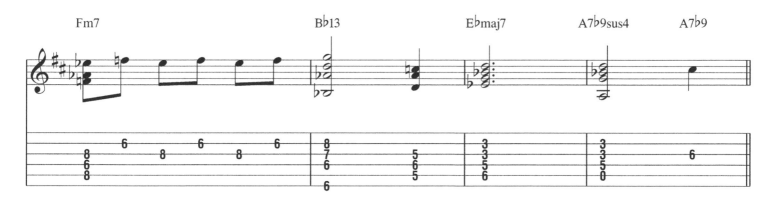

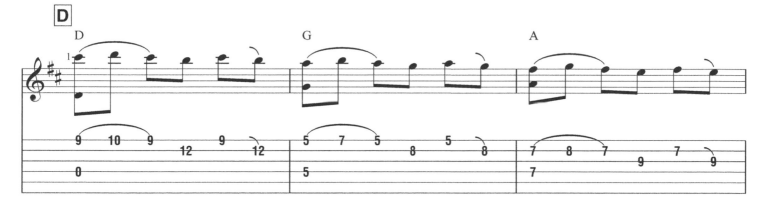

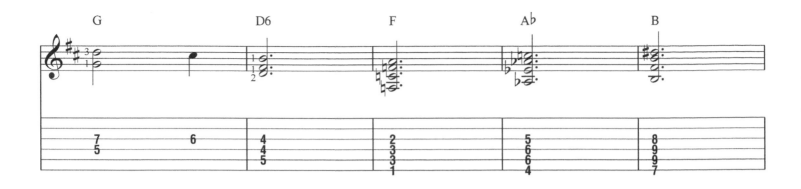

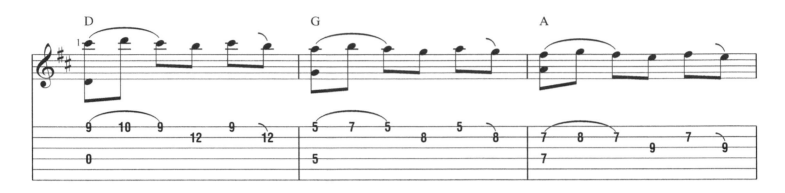

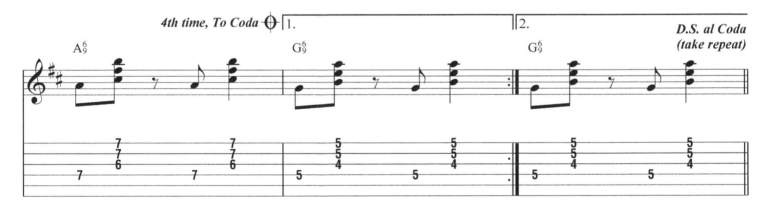

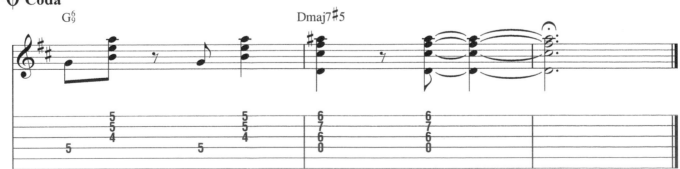

The Star Carol

Lyric by Wihla Hutson
Music by Alfred Burt

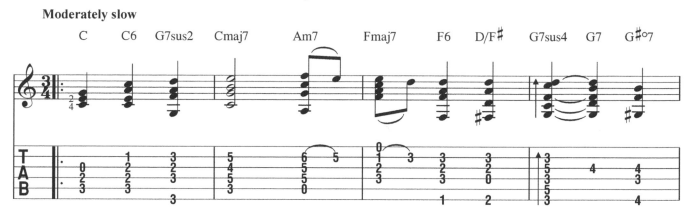

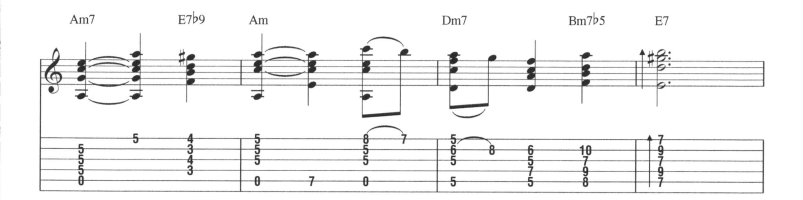

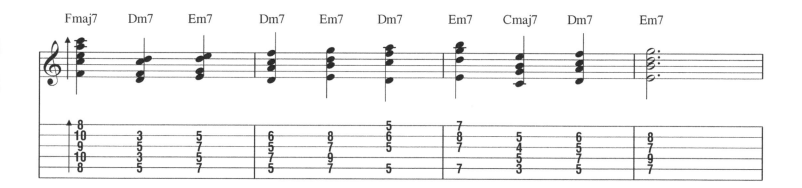

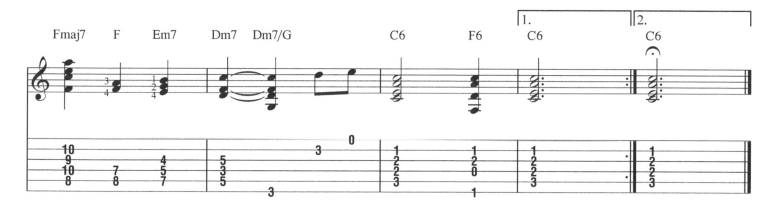

Sleigh Ride

Music by Leroy Anderson

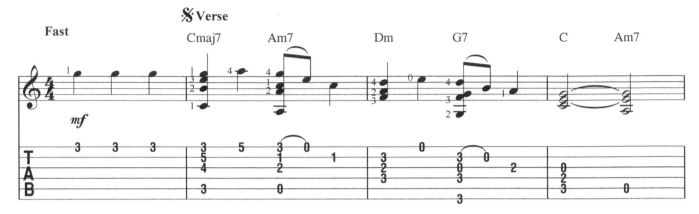

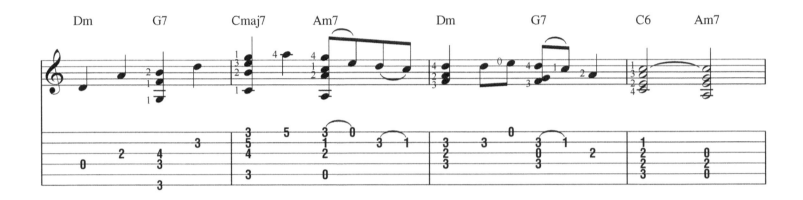

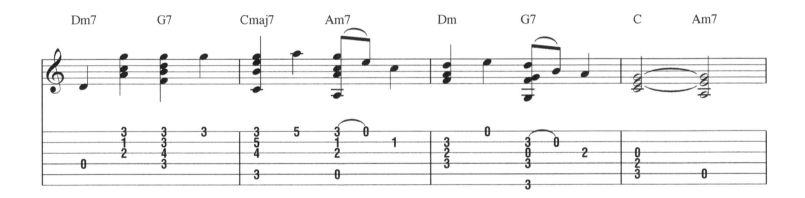

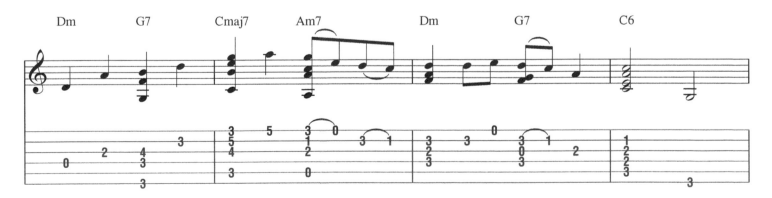

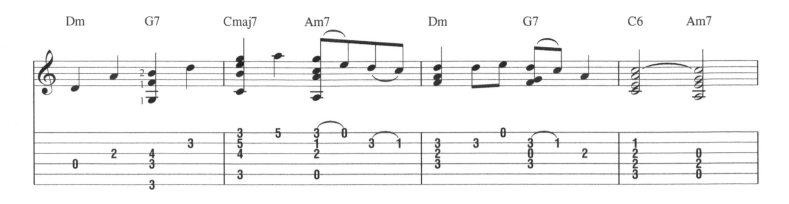

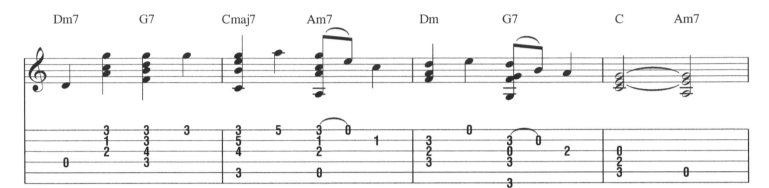

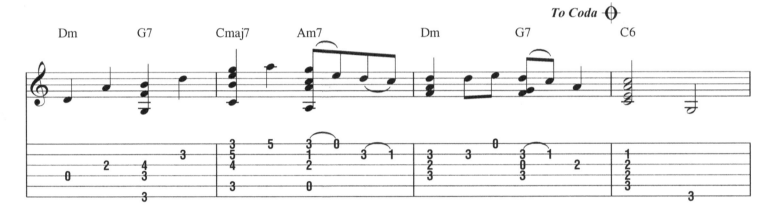

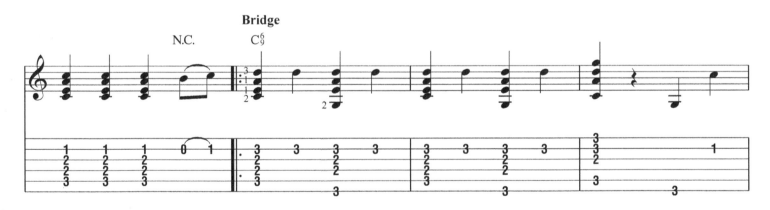

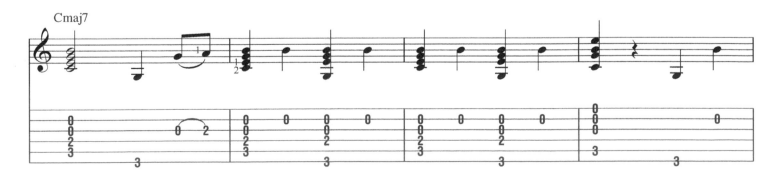

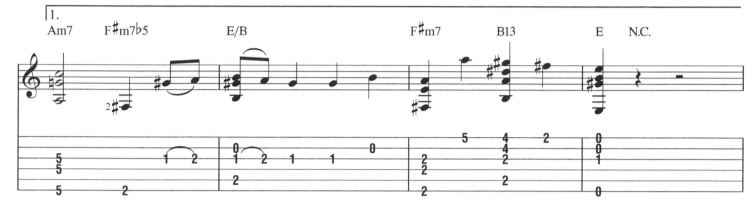

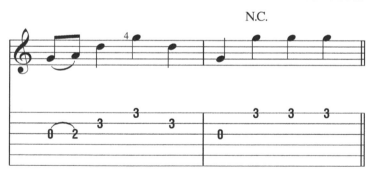

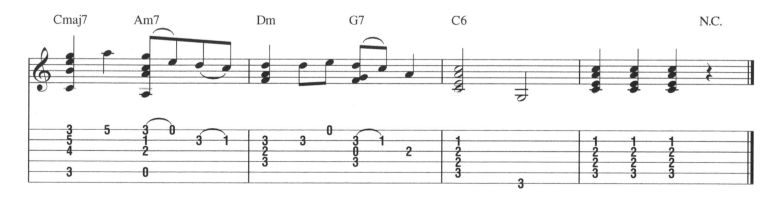

Somewhere in My Memory

from the Twentieth Century Fox Motion Picture HOME ALONE

Words by Leslie Bricusse
Music by John Williams

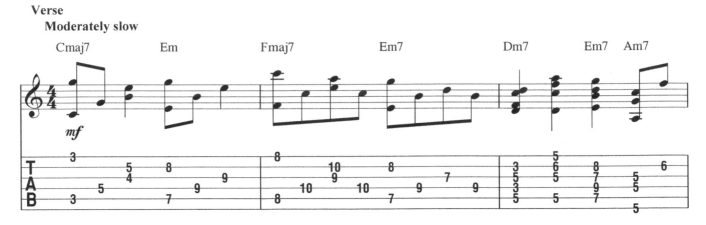

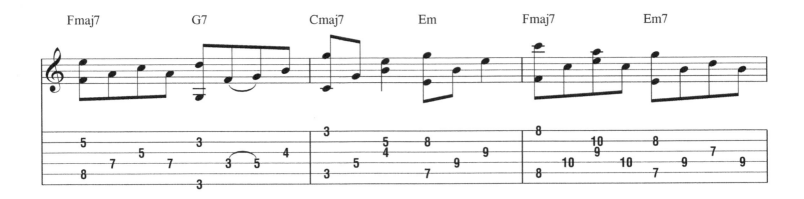

Verse

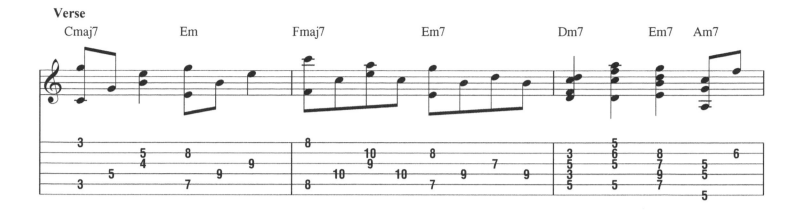

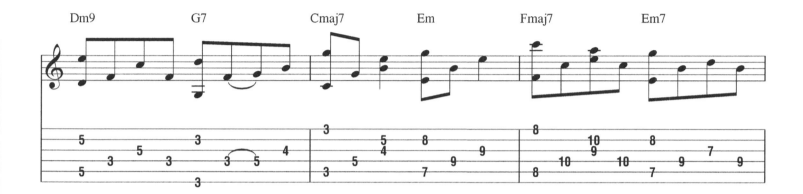

*w/ base segment of 1st finger.

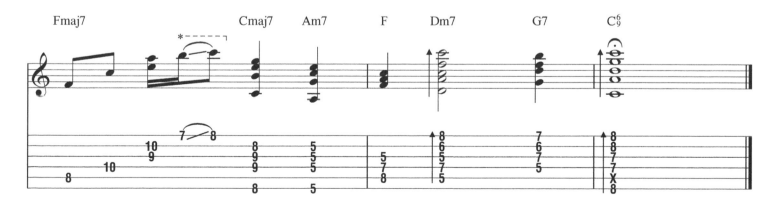

White Christmas

from the Motion Picture Irving Berlin's HOLIDAY INN

Words and Music by Irving Berlin

Verse
Moderately slow

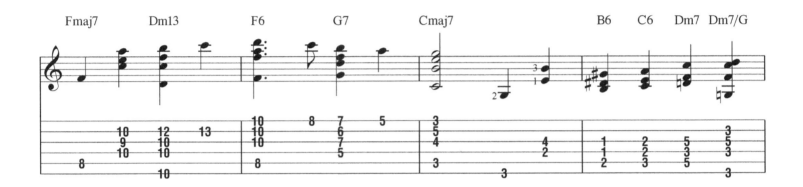

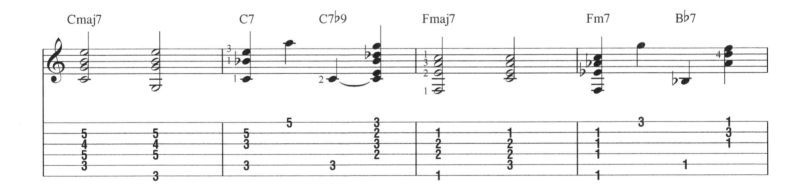

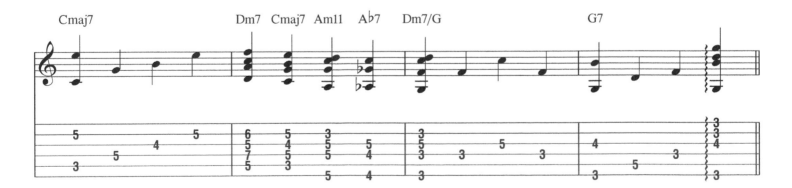

Verse

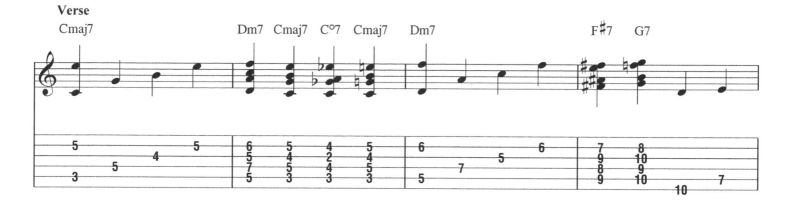

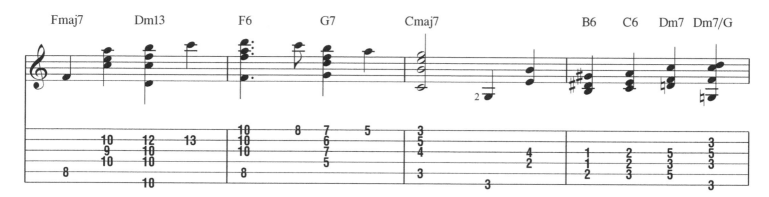

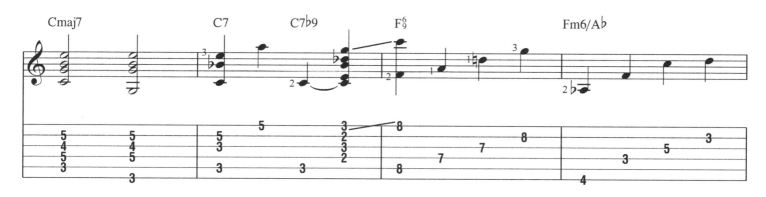

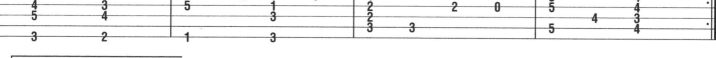

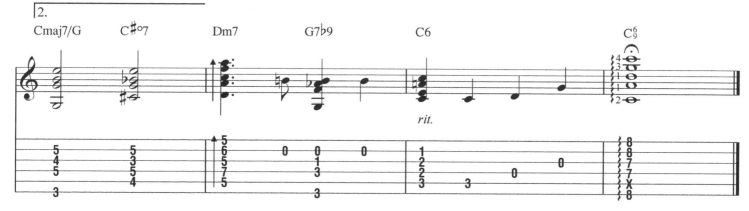

Winter Wonderland

Words by Dick Smith
Music by Felix Bernard

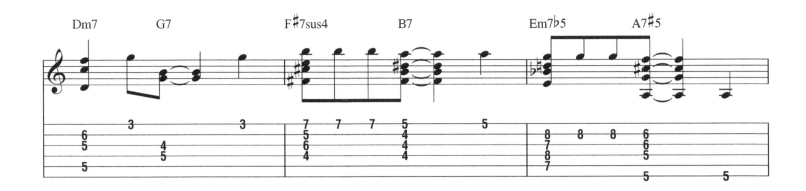

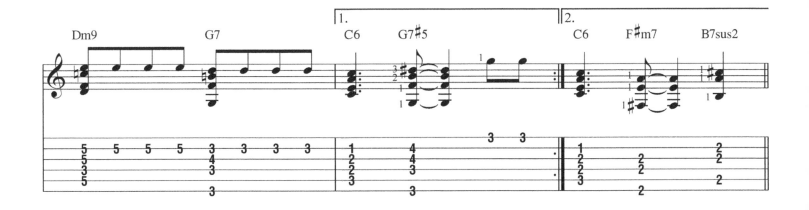

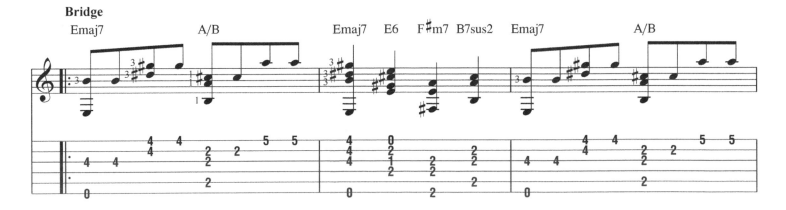

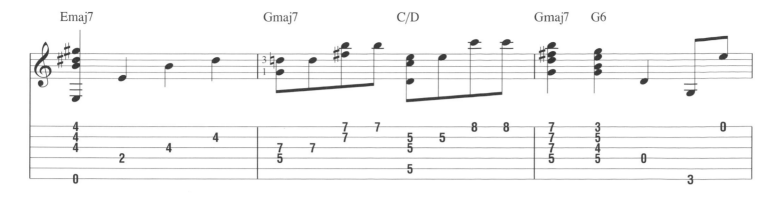

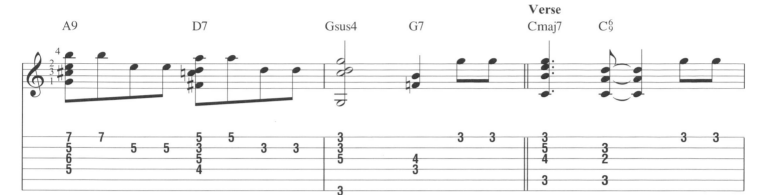

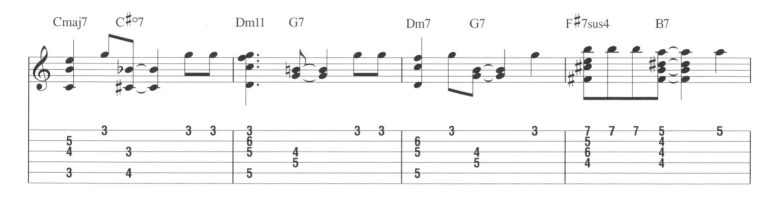

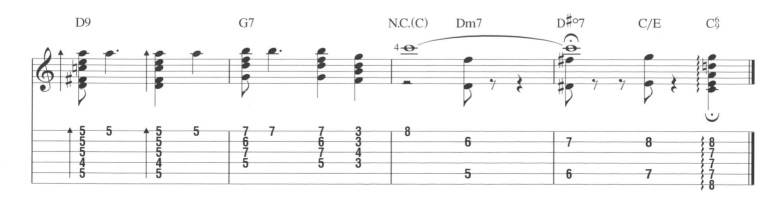

JAZZ GUITAR CHORD MELODY SOLOS

This series features chord melody arrangements in standard notation and tablature of songs for intermediate guitarists. **INCLUDES TAB**

ALL-TIME STANDARDS
27 songs, including: All of Me • Bewitched • Come Fly with Me • A Fine Romance • Georgia on My Mind • How High the Moon • I'll Never Smile Again • I've Got You Under My Skin • It's De-Lovely • It's Only a Paper Moon • My Romance • Satin Doll • The Surrey with the Fringe on Top • Yesterdays • and more.
00699757 Solo Guitar $15.99

IRVING BERLIN
27 songs, including: Alexander's Ragtime Band • Always • Blue Skies • Cheek to Cheek • Easter Parade • Happy Holiday • Heat Wave • How Deep Is the Ocean • Puttin' On the Ritz • Remember • They Say It's Wonderful • What'll I Do? • White Christmas • and more.
00700637 Solo Guitar $14.99

CHRISTMAS CAROLS
26 songs, including: Auld Lang Syne • Away in a Manger • Deck the Hall • God Rest Ye Merry, Gentlemen • Good King Wenceslas • Here We Come A-Wassailing • It Came upon the Midnight Clear • Joy to the World • O Holy Night • O Little Town of Bethlehem • Silent Night • Toyland • We Three Kings of Orient Are • and more.
00701697 Solo Guitar $12.99

CHRISTMAS JAZZ
21 songs, including Auld Lang Syne • Baby, It's Cold Outside • Cool Yule • Have Yourself a Merry Little Christmas • I've Got My Love to Keep Me Warm • Mary, Did You Know? • Santa Baby • Sleigh Ride • White Christmas • Winter Wonderland • and more.
00171334 Solo Guitar $14.99

DISNEY SONGS
27 songs, including: Beauty and the Beast • Can You Feel the Love Tonight • Candle on the Water • Colors of the Wind • A Dream Is a Wish Your Heart Makes • Heigh-Ho • Some Day My Prince Will Come • Under the Sea • When You Wish upon a Star • A Whole New World (Aladdin's Theme) • Zip-A-Dee-Doo-Dah • and more.
00701902 Solo Guitar $14.99

DUKE ELLINGTON
25 songs, including: C-Jam Blues • Caravan • Do Nothin' Till You Hear from Me • Don't Get Around Much Anymore • I Got It Bad and That Ain't Good • I'm Just a Lucky So and So • In a Sentimental Mood • It Don't Mean a Thing (If It Ain't Got That Swing) • Mood Indigo • Perdido • Prelude to a Kiss • Satin Doll • and more.
00700636 Solo Guitar $12.99

FAVORITE STANDARDS
27 songs, including: All the Way • Autumn in New York • Blue Skies • Cheek to Cheek • Don't Get Around Much Anymore • How Deep Is the Ocean • I'll Be Seeing You • Isn't It Romantic? • It Could Happen to You • The Lady Is a Tramp • Moon River • Speak Low • Take the "A" Train • Willow Weep for Me • Witchcraft • and more.
00699756 Solo Guitar $14.99

JAZZ BALLADS
27 songs, including: Body and Soul • Darn That Dream • Easy to Love (You'd Be So Easy to Love) • Here's That Rainy Day • In a Sentimental Mood • Misty • My Foolish Heart • My Funny Valentine • The Nearness of You • Stella by Starlight • Time After Time • The Way You Look Tonight • When Sunny Gets Blue • and more.
00699755 Solo Guitar $14.99

LATIN STANDARDS
27 Latin favorites, including: Água De Beber (Water to Drink) • Desafinado • The Girl from Ipanema • How Insensitive (Insensatez) • Little Boat • Meditation • One Note Samba (Samba De Uma Nota So) • Poinciana • Quiet Nights of Quiet Stars • Samba De Orfeu • So Nice (Summer Samba) • Wave • and more.
00699754 Solo Guitar $14.99

HAL•LEONARD®

www.halleonard.com